Christmas

Eggnog

Cookbook

About the Author

Laura Sommers is **The Recipe Lady!**

She is a loving wife and mother who lives on a small farm in Baltimore County, Maryland and has a passion for all things domestic especially when it comes to saving money. She has a profitable eBay business and is a couponing addict. Follow her tips and tricks to learn how to make delicious meals on a budget, save money or to learn the latest life hack!

Visit her Amazon Author Page to see her latest books:

amazon.com/author/laurasommers

Visit the Recipe Lady's blog for even more great recipes and to learn which books are **FREE** for download each week:

http://the-recipe-lady.blogspot.com/

Follow the Recipe Lady on **Pinterest**:

http://pinterest.com/therecipelady1

Subscribe to The Recipe Lady blog through Amazon and have recipes and updates sent directly to your Kindle:

The Recipe Lady Blog through Amazon

Laura Sommers is also an Extreme Couponer and Penny Hauler! If you would like to find out how to get things for **FREE** with coupons or how to get things for only a **PENNY**, then visit her couponing blog **Penny Items and Freebies**

http://penny-items-and-freebies.blogspot.com/

Other Books by Laura Sommers

- **Christmas Stuffing Recipes**
- **Christmas Hot Chocolate Recipes**
- **Christmas Cookies**
- **Candy Corn Cookbook**
- **Halloween Recipes**
- **50 Pumpkin Recipes**
- **Recipes for Leftover Thanksgiving or Christmas Turkey**

Introduction

Nothing reminds of us of the Christmas Season quite like eggnog.

Eggnog was originally a drink for the aristocracy. Fresh milk and eggs, and sherry and cinnamon and nutmeg were foods and spices of the wealthy, so eggnog was often used to toast prosperity and good health. Those who could afford milk and eggs and costly spirits mixed it the eggnog with brandy, Madeira wine or sherry to make a drink similar to modern alcoholic egg nog.

Today eggnog represents the celebrations of Christmas, Thanksgiving, New Years and the rest of the Holiday season. There are many variations of the drink and it is also used to flavor many holiday dishes. This cookbook is full of delicious decadent eggnog drink recipes as well as eggnog flavored dishes for you to enjoy.

Ambassador's Eggnog Punch

Ingredients:

1 qt. chilled eggnog
5 oz. brandy
4 oz. dark rum
3 oz. dark creme de cacao
1 whole nutmeg

Directions:

1. Whisk together the eggnog, brandy, rum and creme de cacao together in a large punch bowl.
2. Add a large block of ice.
3. Grate a little nutmeg over the top of each drink when serving.

Baltimore Eggnog

Ingredients:

1 oz. Jamaican dark rum
1 oz. brandy
1 oz. madeira
1 whole egg
1 tsp. powdered sugar
3/4 cup milk

Directions:

1. Shake all ingredients well with cracked ice and strain into a collins glass.
2. Sprinkle nutmeg on top and serve.

Bourbon Eggnog

Ingredients:

6 seperated eggs
1 oz. rum
1 cup sugar
1 pint heavy cream
1 pint milk
1 pint bourbon whiskey

Directions:

1. Separate 6 eggs.
2. Beat yolks well. Beat in 1/2 cup sugar.
3. Clean/degrease beaters and bowl.
4. Beat egg whites until stiff peaks form. Beat in 1/2 cup sugar.
5. Fold in yolks to whites.
6. Gently stir in 1 pt. heavy cream, 1 pt. milk, 1 pt. bourbon, and 1 oz. rum. Serve as is or well chilled.
7. Double recipe to fill a punch bowl.

Cognac Eggnog

Ingredients:

12 seperated eggs
3 pints heavy cream
1 cup granulated sugar
grated nutmeg
1 cup bourbon whiskey
1 cup cognac
1/2 tsp salt

Directions:

1. In an electric mixer, beat the egg yolks with the sugar until thick and lemon colored.
2. Slowly add the bourbon and cognac, while beating at a slow speed.
3. Chill several hours.
4. Add the salt to the egg whites and beat until almost stiff, or until the beaten whites form a peak that bends slightly.
5. Whip the cream until stiff.
6. Fold the whipped cream into the yolk mixture, then fold in the beaten egg whites.
7. Chill one hour.
8. When ready to serve, sprinkle the top with freshly grated nutmeg.
9. Serve in punch bowl.
10. If desired, add one or two cups of milk to the yolk mixture for a thinner eggnog.

Apricot Brandy Eggnog

Ingredients:

6 large eggs
Freshly ground nutmeg
1 cup powdered sugar
750 ml. dark rum
4 cups whipping cream
1/2 cup apricot brandy

Directions:

1. Separate eggs and refrigerate the whites.
2. Beat yolks until light in color.
3. Gradually beat in sugar, then slowly beat in 1 cup of rum.
4. Let stand covered for at least 1 hour.
5. Add rest of liquor, cream, and apricot brandy, beating constantly. Refrigerate, covered, for 3 hours.
6. Beat egg whites until stiff, fold in.
7. Serve sprinkled with nutmeg.
8. Serve in a punch bowl or another medium sized bowl.

Vanilla Eggnog

Ingredients:

6 egg yolks
1 tsp vanilla
Ground nutmeg
1/4 cup sugar
1/4 tsp salt
2 cups milk
1 cup whipping cream
1/2 cup light rum
6 egg whites
1/2 cup bourbon whiskey
1/4 cup sugar

Directions:

1. In a small mixer bowl beat egg yolks till blended.
2. Gradually add 1/4 cup sugar, beating at high speed till thick and lemon colored.
3. Stir in milk, stir in rum, bourbon, vanilla, and salt.
4. Chill thoroughly.
5. Whip cream. Wash beaters well. In a large mixer bowl beat egg whites till soft peaks form.
6. Gradually add remaining 1/4 cup sugar, beating to stiff peaks.
7. Fold yolk mixture and whipped cream into egg whites.
8. Sprinkle nutmeg over each serving.

Cooked Hazelnut Eggnog

Ingredients:

1 cup granulated sugar
1/2 tsp vanilla
1 tbsp sugar
1/2 cup water
1/8 tsp nutmeg
1/2 tsp lemon juice
1/8 tsp salt
6 eggs
3/4 cup heavy cream
4 cups milk
2 tbsp. hazelnut liqueur

Directions:

1. Here's an egg nog recipe using cooked eggs, so no one has to be paranoid about salmonella.
2. Mix granulated sugar, 2 tbsp. of water, and lemon juice in a med. sized sauce pan.
3. Let boil, cook 5 min, until it turns dark amber.
4. Remove from heat, and slowly stir in remaining 1/4 c. of water.
5. Beat eggs and milk together in a bowl. Stir into sugar mixture, cook over med.-low heat for about 10 to 12 minutes.
6. It should thicken enough to stick to spoon.
7. Poor into a punch bowl.
8. Stir in vanilla, nutmeg and salt.
9. Refrigerate, covered, until cold.
10. Before serving, beat together cream, liqueur, and 10x sugar, until soft peaks form.
11. Pour chilled eggnog into a serving bowl, fold in whipped cream with a whisk.

Healthy Eggnog

Ingredients:

3 oz. rum
3 tbsp. sugar
nutmeg
13 oz. skimmed condensed milk
3/4 cup skimmed milk
1 tsp vanilla

Directions:

1. Whip egg substitute and sugar together, combine with the two kinds of milk, vanilla, and rum.
2. Mix well.
3. Chill overnight.
4. Sprinkle with nutmeg.

Kahlua Eggnog

Ingredients:

1 oz. Kahlua® coffee liqueur
4 oz. eggnog
Nutmeg

Directions:

1. Mix Kahlua with eggnog in a wine glass and then sprinkle nutmeg on top.

Peach Eggnog

Ingredients:

12 separated eggs
2 qt. milk
1 1/2 cups powdered sugar
1 qt. half-and-half
1 pint rye whiskey
1 pint heavy cream
1/3 pint rum
1/4 pint peach liqueur

Directions:

1. Beat egg yolks until thick and lemon yellow, then beat in 1 cup sugar. Add slowly the rye, rum and peach liqueur. Beat until smooth.
2. Add the milk and half-and-half.
3. Beat the egg whites until stiff but not dry, gradually adding 1/2 cup of confectioners' sugar.
4. Fold the egg whites into the batter.
5. Just before serving, whip the cream and fold it into the other ingredients.
6. Garnish with ground nutmeg.
7. Serve in a punch bowl or another big bowl.

Williamsburg Eggnog

Ingredients:

6 eggs
1/2 cup rum
2 cups heavy cream
1/2 cup brandy
1 cup milk
1/2 cup whisky
3/4 - 1 cup sugar
1 tbsp. nutmeg

Directions:

1. Separate the eggs, yolks and whites.
2. Set the white aside. Mix yolks well, gradually adding the cream, milk, and sugar.
3. Whip the egg whites until soft peaks form.
4. Fold the white into the rest.
5. Gradually add the alcohol.
6. Either add nutmeg right away, or sprinkle on top later.
7. Age for at least 2 hours in refrigerator, uncovered.

Classic Cooked Eggnog

Ingredients:

6 eggs
1/4 cup sugar
1/4 tsp salt
1 qt. milk
1 tsp vanilla

Directions:

1. In large saucepan, beat together eggs, sugar and salt, if desired.
2. Stir in 2 cups of the milk.
3. Cook over low heat, stirring constantly, until mixture is thick enough to coat a metal spoon and reaches 160 degrees F.
4. Remove from heat.
5. Stir in remaining 2 cups milk and vanilla.
6. Cover and refrigerate until thoroughly chilled, several hours or overnight. Just before serving, pour into bowl or pitcher.
7. Garnish or add stir-ins, if desired.
8. Choose 1 or several of the following for garnish: Chocolate curls, cinnamon sticks, extracts of flavorings, flavored brandy or liqueur, fruit juice or nectar, ground nutmeg, maraschino cherries, orange slices, peppermint sticks or candy canes, plain brandy, run or whiskey, sherbet, ice-cream or whipped cream.

Kentucky Eggnog

Ingredients:

1 qt. whipped heavy cream
6 eggs
1 cup sugar
2 cups bourbon whiskey

Directions:

1. Separate eggs.
2. Beat yolks, add sugar.
3. Add bourbon slowly while beating.
4. Beat egg whites until stiff.
5. Fold whites into egg yolk mixture, then fold whipped cream into mixture. Refrigerate for more than 4 days.
6. Stir frequently to avoid separation.
7. Color will change to a pale color.
8. Serve with nutmeg or cinnamon.

Spiked Eggnog

Ingredients:

12 eggs
3 pints heavy cream
1 cup sugar
1/2 tsp nutmeg
1 cup bourbon whiskey
1 cup cognac
1/2 tsp salt

Directions:

1. Separate the eggs. In an electric mixer, beat the egg yolks with the sugar until thick and lemon colored.
2. Slowly add the bourbon and cognac, while beating at slow speed.
3. Chill several hours.
4. Add the salt to the egg whites and beat until almost stiff, or until the beaten whites form a peak that bends slightly.
5. Whip the cream until stiff.
6. Fold the whipped cream into the yolk mixture, then fold in the beaten egg whites.
7. Chill one hour.
8. When ready to serve, sprinkle the top with freshly grated nutmeg.

Golden Blizzard Eggnog

Ingredients:

1 1/2 cups eggnog
2 shots Goldschlager® cinnamon schnapps
2 shots peppermint schnapps

Directions:

1. Add the shots of goldschlager and peppermint schnapps to a mason jar.
2. Fill with eggnog.

Good Morning Eggnog

Ingredients:

1 3/4 oz. ruby port
1 3/4 oz. red wine
3 1/2 oz. milk
3/4 oz. cream
1/2 tsp powdered sugar
1 egg yolk
1 pinch nutmeg

Directions:

1. Shake well over ice cubes in a shaker, and strain into a large highball glass over ice cubes.
2. Sprinkle with nutmeg, and serve.

Granny's Eggnog

Ingredients:

6 egg yolks
Nutmeg
1/2 cup granulated sugar
2 cups milk
2 cups light rum
2 cups whipping cream

Directions:

1. Beat yolks until light.
2. Add sugar and mix well. Add milk and rum.
3. Mix well, then chill for at least 3 hours.
4. One hour before serving, whip cream and stir into chilled mixture. Return to refrigerator for an hour.
5. Serve in punch cups and dust with nutmeg. Serves 20

Holiday Eggnog

Ingredients:

6 oz. rum
6 oz. bourbon whiskey
6 beaten eggs
6 oz. sugar
1/2 tsp salt
15 oz. whipping cream
15 oz. milk

Directions:

1. Mix ingredients in a punch bowl until sugar dissolves.
2. Chill for five hours.
3. Mix, and sprinkle with grated nutmeg.
4. Serve.

Peppermint Eggnog Punch

Ingredients:

1 quart peppermint ice cream
1 quart eggnog
4 (12 fluid oz.) cans or bottles ginger ale, chilled
1 cup rum
24 small peppermint candy canes for garnish

Directions:

1. Set aside 2 or 3 round scoops of ice cream in the freezer for garnish.
2. Stir remaining ice cream until softened.
3. Gradually stir in eggnog and rum.
4. Transfer to a punch bowl, and stir in ginger ale.
5. Hang candy canes around the edge of the punchbowl.
6. Float reserved ice cream scoops on top, and serve immediately.

Cranberry Eggnog

Ingredients:

1/2 cup cranberries
1 cup water
1/2 cup white sugar
1 tsp. ground nutmeg
1 quart eggnog

Directions:

1. In a small saucepan over medium heat, combine cranberries and water.
2. Bring to a boil and cook until the cranberries are mushy.
3. Stir in sugar and nutmeg; remove from heat.
4. Pour the eggnog into a blender along with the cranberry mixture and mix until well blended.

Amaretto Eggnog

Ingredients:

1 cup eggnog
1 (1.5 fluid oz.) jigger amaretto liqueur

Directions:

1. Pour eggnog into a microwave-safe mug.
2. Heat in the microwave until warmed through, 30 seconds to 1 minute.
3. Stir in amaretto liqueur.

Hot Eggnog

Ingredients:

1/2 oz. brandy
1/2 oz. dark rum
1/2 oz. sugar syrup
1 egg
3 oz. boiling milk

Directions:

1. Blend all ingredients (except milk) until smooth and pour into a heat-proof goblet.
2. Add boiling milk, sprinkle with nutmeg and serve.

Jager Eggnog

Ingredients:

3 parts eggnog
1 part Jagermeister® herbal liqueur

Directions:

1. Mix in a punchbowl or make individual drinks.

Kahlua Almond Eggnog

1 oz. amaretto almond liqueur
1/4 oz. Kahlua coffee liqueur
5 oz. eggnog
1 shot whipped cream

Directions:

1. Pour eggnog into a coffee mug. Stir in amaretto, and float Kahlua on top.
2. Add a small shot of whipped cream, then sprinkle a couple of pinches of nutmeg on top.

Rum Eggnog

Ingredients:

2 oz. light rum
6 oz. milk
1 tsp powdered sugar
1 whole egg
Nutmeg

Directions:

1. Shake all ingredients (except nutmeg) with ice and strain into a collins glass.
2. Sprinkle nutmeg on top and serve.

Schlag Nog recipe

Ingredients:

3 parts eggnog
1 part Goldschlager® cinnamon schnapps
Ground nutmeg

Directions:

1. Add the egg nog and Goldschlager together in a bowl.
2. Add nutmeg if desired.

Sherry Eggnog recipe

Ingredients:

2 oz. sherry
1 tsp powdered sugar
1 whole egg
Milk
Nutmeg

Directions:

1. Shake sherry, powdered sugar, and egg with ice and strain into a collins glass.
2. Fill with milk and stir.
3. Sprinkle nutmeg on top and serve.

Snowboard Eggnog

Ingredients:

3 cl. vodka
3 cl. eggnog
Soda water
Crushed ice
1 slice kiwi

Directions:

1. Mix everything together in the glass.
2. Add enough soda water to fill the rest of the glass.
3. The drink is best if the ice is like slush.
4. Serve with a slice of kiwi.

Waldorf Astoria Eggnog

Ingredients:

2 egg yolks
1/4 oz. cream
1/2 oz. sugar syrup
Nutmeg
3/4 oz. tawny port
1 1/2 oz. bourbon whiskey
3 1/2 oz. milk

Directions:

1. Shake well over ice cubes in a shaker and strain into a large highball glass over ice cubes.
2. Sprinkle with nutmeg.

Whiskey Eggnog

Ingredients:

2 oz. blended whiskey
1 tsp. powdered sugar
1 whole egg
5 oz. milk
Nutmeg

Directions:

1. Shake all ingredients (except nutmeg) with ice and strain into a collins glass.
2. Sprinkle nutmeg on top and serve.

Pumpkin Spice Eggnog

Ingredients:

4 egg yolks
1/3 cup white sugar
1/3 cup pumpkin puree
2 cups milk
1 cup heavy cream
½ tsp. vanilla extract
1 tsp. freshly grated nutmeg
½ tsp. pumpkin pie spice

Directions:

1. Pour egg yolks into the bowl of a stand mixer and mix on medium speed.
2. Add sugar slowly and continue mixing until just combined.
3. Adjust mixer speed to low and add in pumpkin, milk, cream, vanilla, nutmeg, and pumpkin pie spice.
4. Pour into a pitcher and chill before serving.

Pumpkin Eggnog with Bourbon

Ingredients:

8 egg yolks
1 1/2 cups whole milk
1 1/2 cups cream
1 cup granulated sugar
A pinch of salt
2 tsps. vanilla extract
1/4 cup bourbon or dark rum
1/4 cup + 1 tbsp. pumpkin puree
1/2 tsp. ground cinnamon
1/4 tsp. ground ginger
A pinch of ground cloves
1/4 tsp. grated nutmeg, plus more to garnish

Directions:

1. Place the yolks into a blender.
2. In a medium heavy bottomed saucepan, bring the milk, cream, sugar and salt to a simmer over medium heat. Do not let boil.
3. Give the eggs a quick pulse in the blender to combine.
4. With the blender on, slowly add half of the hot milk mixture to the egg yolks.
5. Once combined, pour the egg-milk mixture back into the saucepan set over medium heat.
6. Whisk mixture constantly and cook until it starts to thicken and mixture reaches 160F on a thermometer (about 3-5 minutes).
7. Remove from heat and which in the vanilla extract, bourbon, pumpkin, cinnamon, ginger cloves and nutmeg.
8. Strain through a fine mesh sifter and chill for 2-3 hours before serving.
9. Serve chilled with additional nutmeg.

Peppermint Eggnog

Ingredients:

6 large eggs
2 large egg yolks
1/2 cup sugar
2 tbsps. more sugar
1/4 tsp. salt
1/2 tsp. pure peppermint extract
1 tbsp. pure vanilla extract
4 cups whole milk
12 peppermint candy canes, broken into pieces
3 oz. white chocolate, coarsely chopped
1/2 cup heavy cream
Peppermint sticks, for garnish

Directions:

1. Prepare an ice-water bath; set aside. Whisk together eggs, egg yolks, sugar, salt, and the extracts in large saucepan over medium-low heat until combined.
2. Pour in milk in a slow, steady stream, whisking until fully incorporated. Raise heat to medium.
3. Cook, whisking constantly, until mixture registers 160 degrees on an instant-read thermometer and is thick enough to coat the back of a spoon, 30 to 35 minutes.
4. Pour milk mixture through a fine sieve into a medium bowl. Set bowl in ice-water bath; let mixture cool completely.
5. Transfer custard to an airtight container, and refrigerate at least 4 hours or up to overnight.
6. Process candy canes in a food processor until finely crushed.
7. Sift in a strainer to discard dust. Transfer to a shallow dish.
8. Melt chocolate in a heatproof bowl set over a pan of simmering water. Let cool 5 minutes.
9. Dip rim of each cup into melted chocolate, then crushed peppermint. Refrigerate until set, about 5 minutes.
10. Remove custard from refrigerator; set aside.
11. Put cream into the bowl of an electric mixer fitted with the whisk attachment; mix on medium speed until stiff peaks form.
12. Fold into cold custard until combined. Fill cups with eggnog.
13. Sprinkle with crushed peppermint, and garnish with peppermint sticks.
14. Serve and enjoy!

Coquito - Puerto Rican Coconut Eggnog

Ingredients:

1 (12-oz.) can evaporated milk
2 large egg yolks
1 (15-oz.) can unsweetened coconut milk
1 (14-oz.) can sweetened condensed milk
1 cup white rum
1/4 tsp. ground cinnamon
1 pinch of salt

Directions:

1. Beat together the evaporated milk and egg yolks in a medium bowl.
2. Strain into a 3-quart pot and simmer over medium heat until slightly thickened, about 5 minutes.
3. Remove from the heat and let cool.
4. Transfer the egg yolk mixture to a blender, and blend in batches.
5. Add the remaining ingredients, blending at high speed until frothy.
6. Pour into a pitcher and refrigerate until chilled before serving.

Russian Eggnog

Ingredients:

1/2 (1.5 fluid oz.) jigger spiced rum
1 (1.5 fluid oz.) jigger coffee flavored liqueur
3/4 cup eggnog
1 pinch ground nutmeg

Directions:

1. Pour the spiced rum and coffee liqueur into a glass.
2. Top with eggnog.
3. Stir and sprinkle some nutmeg on the top.

Texas Farm Eggnog

Ingredients:

2 1/2 oz. sherry (nutty)
2 oz. tequila
3 oz. sugar
2 whole eggs (farm)
6 oz. milk (raw)
4 oz. heavy cream
1 pinch nutmeg
1 pinch cinnamon
1 pinch salt
1 pinch pepper
Nutmeg
Star anise

Directions:

1. Combine all ingredients in a blender starting with eggs and ending with heavy cream.
2. Refrigerate for two days.
3. Garnish with grated nutmeg and star anise.

White Christmas Eggnog

Ingredients:

4 oz. eggnog
1/2 oz. white chocolate liqueur
1 oz. Southern Comfort
Edible gold or chocolate flakes for garnish

Directions:

1. Build the ingredients in a snifter glass and stir lightly.
2. Sprinkle gold or chocolate flakes on top.

Vegan Eggnog

Ingredients:

21 oz. tofu (extra-firm silken)
2 cups soymilk
2/3 cup turbinado sugar or light brown sugar
1/4 tsp. salt
1 cup water, cold
1 cup rum or brandy
4 1/2 tsp. vanilla extract
20 ice cubes
Nutmeg for garnish

Directions:

1. Place the crumbled tofu and soymilk in a blender with the sugar and salt.
2. Blend until very smooth.
3. Scrape this into a large bowl or pitcher, and whisk in the water, rum or brandy and vanilla.
4. Mix well, cover and refrigerate until serving time.
5. To serve, blend half of the mixture in the blender with 10 of the ice cubes until frothy.
6. Repeat with the other half.
7. Serve in glasses with nutmeg sprinkled on top.

Canlis Seattle Highland Eggnog

Ingredients:

1 1/2 oz. Famous Grouse (Or Macallan 12)
1/2 oz. Zirbenz (Austrian stone pine liqueur)
3/4 oz. brown sugar syrup (2 to 1 ratio)
1 whole egg
1 1/4 oz. heavy cream

Directions:

1. Measure off the spirits and syrup in a small measuring cup.
2. Separate the egg white from the yolk, saving the yolk.
3. In the mixing glass whip the egg white with a hand blender for 20 seconds.
4. Add the yolk and continue whipping for 10 seconds.
5. Now add the spirits and syrup from the measuring cup.
6. Once incorporated, add the heavy cream whipping until froth forms.
7. Add ice to the mixing glass and shake for 15 seconds until the outside of the shaker is cold.
8. Pour contents into a long drink glass.
9. Garnish with fresh ground nutmeg and a sprig from your favorite evergreen tree.

Eggnog Hot Chocolate

Ingredients:

2 1/2 cups milk
12 oz. bittersweet chocolate chips
4 cups eggnog
1 tsp. vanilla extract
1/4 cup coffee flavored liqueur
whipped cream
8 cinnamon sticks, garnish

Directions:

1. In a medium saucepan, melt chocolate in milk over medium-low heat. Remove from heat, and let stand for 2 minutes.
2. Whisk the chocolate until melted and smooth.
3. Stir in the eggnog, and heat gently over low heat until very warm but not boiling.
4. Remove from heat, and stir in the vanilla and coffee liqueur.
5. Pour into mugs, and serve with whipped cream and a cinnamon stick garnish.

Bourbon Eggnog Pudding

Ingredients:

3 cups egg nog
1/2 cup sugar
1/3 cup cornstarch
1 pinch salt
1/4 cup bourbon
Nutmeg

Directions:

1. Mix the dry ingredients in a pot and put it on low heat.
2. Whisk in the egg nog and cook for about 10 minutes whisking occasionally until it coats the back of a spoon.
3. Remove from heat and stir in bourbon.
4. Pour into serving cups, cover, and chill until thickened.
5. Sprinkle with nutmeg before serving.

Chocolate Eggnog Pudding

Ingredients:

3/4 cup milk
1 pkg. instant chocolate pudding mix
1 1/4 cups eggnog
1/2 cup whipping cream
Chocolate sprinkles

Directions:

1. Stir milk into pudding in small bowl.
2. Beat with rotary beater until blended.
3. Slowly add egg nog, beating until very smooth, about 1 minute.
4. Pour into 4 sherbet glasses; refrigerate until serving time.
5. Top with whipped whipping cream and chocolate sprinkles.

Eggnog Truffles

Ingredients:

2 cups/12 oz. chopped white chocolate or chocolate chips
1/8 tsp. salt
4 tbsps./2 oz. butter (room temperature)
1/3 cup eggnog
1/4 to 1/2 tsp. nutmeg (plus more to decorate)
12 oz. white chocolate candy coating
1/4 cup powdered sugar

Directions:

1. In a medium bowl, combine the white chocolate, the salt, and the butter.
2. Place the eggnog in a small saucepan over medium-high heat and bring it to a simmer.
3. Once the eggnog is simmering and bubbles are forming around the edges of the pan, pour the hot eggnog over the white chocolate.
4. Let it sit for a minute to soften the chocolate, then gently whisk everything together until the chocolate is dissolved and the mixture is smooth and free of lumps.
5. If there are pockets of chocolate that won't dissolve, microwave the mixture in 6-second intervals, whisking well after each one, just until the chocolate dissolves.
6. Add 1/4 tsp of nutmeg and whisk it in. Once incorporated, taste the ganache, and add an additional 1/4 tsp nutmeg if desired.
7. Press a layer of cling wrap on top of the ganache, and refrigerate it until firm enough to scoop, at least 2 hours.
8. Once firm, use a spoon or a small candy scoop to form the truffle mixture into small 1-inch balls.
9. Roll the balls between your palms to make them round.
10. If they start to get sticky, dust your palms with the 1/4 cup of powdered sugar periodically to keep them from sticking.
11. Place the rolled truffles on a foil-covered baking sheet.
12. Melt the white chocolate candy coating in the microwave until it is fluid and free of lumps.
13. Use a fork or dipping tools to dip the truffles one by one into the coating.
14. Let excess coating drip back into the bowl, then place the truffle back on the foil-covered baking sheet.
15. While the coating is still wet, sprinkle the top of the truffles with a light dusting of nutmeg, if desired.
16. Once all the truffles are dipped, let the coating set completely.

Rice Eggnog Pudding

Ingredients:

1 cup, uncooked Texmati White Rice
3 cups eggnog
1 cup evaporated milk
1/2 cup granulated sugar
2 tbsps. granulated sugar
3 eggs, lightly beaten
1 tsp. vanilla
Sprinkling of cinnamon and/or nutmeg

Directions:

1. Prepare rice according to package directions.
2. In a large saucepan combine eggnog, milk, ½ cup sugar, and cooked rice stirring constantly over med-high heat. Bring to a boil. Remove from heat.
3. In a small bowl stir together eggs and 2 tbsps. sugar.
4. Temper eggs by stirring 1/8 cup of milk mixture into the eggs, add this mixture to milk mixture and return to a boil.
5. Remove from heat.
6. Stir in vanilla.
7. Serve with a sprinkling of cinnamon and/or nutmeg.

Eggnog Bread Pudding

Ingredients:

2 cups Eggnog
1 cup sugar
2 eggs
1 tsp nutmeg
1 tsp vanilla extract
8 slices raisin bread cut into 1-inch slices

Whipped Cream Topping Ingredients:

1 cup Kemps Whipping Cream
3 tbsp. powdered sugar
1 tsp. brandy or rum extract

Directions:

1. Heat oven to 350 degrees F.
2. Spray a 2-quart baking dish with vegetable cooking spray.
3. In a large bowl, combine eggnog, sugar, eggs, nutmeg, and vanilla.
4. Blend until smooth.
5. Fold in bread cubes.
6. Pour into prepared dish.
7. Bake for 40-45 minutes, or until knife inserted comes out clean.
8. Serve warm, topped with whipped cream topping.

Eggnog Pound Cake

Ingredients:

1 (16-oz.) pkg. pound cake mix
1 1/4 cups eggnog
2 large eggs
1/2 tsp. freshly grated nutmeg
1/2 tsp. vanilla extract

Directions:

1. Preheat oven to 350 degrees F.
2. Beat all ingredients together at low speed with an electric mixer until blended.
3. Increase speed to medium, and beat 2 minutes.
4. Pour into a lightly greased 9- x 5-inch loaf pan.
5. Bake at 350 degrees F for 1 hour to 1 hour and 5 minutes or until a long wooden pick inserted in center comes out clean.
6. Cool in pan on a wire rack 10 minutes.
7. Remove from pan to wire rack, and cool completely (about 1 hour).

Eggnog Pancakes

Ingredients:

2 tsps. vegetable oil, or as needed
1 cup all-purpose flour
1 tbsp. white sugar
1 tsp. baking powder
1/2 tsp. baking soda
1/4 tsp. salt
1 1/4 cups eggnog

Directions:

1. Heat vegetable oil in a griddle or shallow frying pan over medium heat.
2. Whisk flour, sugar, baking powder, baking soda, and salt together in a bowl; stir eggnog into flour mixture until batter is smooth.
3. Pour enough batter into the heated griddle to make a 4- to 5-inch circle.
4. Cook until bubbles appear around the edges and bottom is browned, about 5 minutes.
5. Flip and cook until other side is evenly browned, about 5 more minutes.
6. Repeat with remaining batter.

Eggnog Custard

Ingredients:

1 egg, beaten
1 cup eggnog
2 tbsps. white sugar
2 pinches ground nutmeg

Directions:

1. Preheat oven to 350 degrees F (175 degrees C).
2. Fill an 8x8 inch baking dish with 1 inch of water.
3. Beat the egg, eggnog, and sugar together in a bowl.
4. Pour into two small baking dishes.
5. Sprinkle tops with nutmeg.
6. Place the baking dishes into the dish with the water.
7. Add more water if necessary to reach halfway up the sides of the baking dishes.
8. Bake in preheated oven until tops are set, 35 to 45 minutes.
9. Cool before serving.

Eggnog Ice Cream

Ingredients:

2 cups eggnog
1 cup heavy whipping cream
1 cup milk

Directions:

1. Mix the eggnog, whipping cream, and milk together in a bowl, and pour the mixture into the freezer container of an ice cream maker.
2. Freeze according to manufacturer's directions.
3. Once frozen, spoon the ice cream into a container, and freeze 2 hours more.

Eggnog Creme Brulee

Ingredients:

2 cups eggnog
4 egg yolks
1/4 cup white sugar
3 oz. mascarpone cheese, softened
1 dash ground nutmeg
1 dash ground cinnamon
1 tsp. vanilla extract

Directions:

1. Preheat oven to 350 degrees F (175 degrees C).
2. Place 4 ramekins or custard cups into a shallow baking dish, and fill the dish with water to half-way up the sides of the ramekins.
3. Pour the eggnog into a pan over medium heat.
4. Cook and stir occasionally until the mixture simmers, about 10 minutes.
5. Meanwhile, place the egg yolks and sugar into a mixing bowl; beat until light colored and frothy.
6. Stir in the mascarpone until well blended and smooth.
7. Whisk 1/4 cup of the heated eggnog mixture into the eggs.
8. Gradually whisk the remaining eggnog into the eggs.
9. Pour the mixture through a fine sieve to remove any egg strands. If desired, stir in the nutmeg, cinnamon, and vanilla.
10. Pour into the prepared ramekins, dividing evenly.
11. Bake in preheated oven until custard has set, 30 to 45 minutes.
12. Centers should wiggle slightly when shaken, but not be soupy.
13. Remove from oven and cool 30 minutes; refrigerate at least 3 hours before serving.

Overnight Eggnog French Toast

Ingredients:

1 cup brown sugar
1/2 cup butter
2 tbsps. corn syrup
1 loaf French bread, cut into
1-inch slices
8 eggs
2 cups prepared eggnog

Directions:

1. Heat the brown sugar, butter, and corn syrup in a small saucepan over medium heat. Cook and stir until the mixture begins to boil; remove the mixture from heat, and pour into the prepared baking dish.
2. Place the bread slices atop the brown sugar mixture.
3. Whisk the eggs and eggnog together in a large bowl; pour over the bread slices.
4. Cover the baking dish with aluminum foil, and refrigerate 8 hours to overnight.
5. Preheat an oven to 325 degrees F (165 degrees C).
6. Remove the baking dish from the refrigerator.
7. Bake in the preheated oven for 35 minutes.
8. Increase heat to 375 degrees F (190 degrees C).
9. Remove the aluminum foil, and continue baking until the top begins to brown, 5 to 7 minutes more.

Cranberry Eggnog Cornbread Scones

Ingredients:

2 cups all-purpose flour
1/2 cup cornmeal
1/3 cup white sugar
1 tbsp. baking powder
1/2 tsp. salt
1/3 cup butter, chilled
3/4 cup craisins (sweetened, dried cranberries)
2/3 cup eggnog

Directions:

1. Preheat oven to 375 degrees F (190 degrees C).
2. Lightly grease a baking sheet.
3. Stir the flour, cornmeal, sugar, baking powder, and salt together in a mixing bowl until blended.
4. Cut in the butter using a pastry cutter or two knives until coarse crumbs form.
5. Mix in the craisins.
6. Use a fork to stir in the eggnog and make a sticky dough.
7. Turn the dough out onto a lightly floured surface.
8. Dip hands in flour and knead the dough about 10 times.
9. Pat the dough out into a disk about 1/2 inch thick. Dip a 2 inch diameter biscuit cutter into some flour, and cut out 8 to 10 rounds.
10. Place rounds about 2 inches apart on prepared baking sheet.
11. Use up remaining dough by patting it into a smaller disk and cutting again.
12. Bake in preheated oven until risen and golden brown, about 15 minutes. Serve warm or at room temperature.

Eggnog Pancakes

Ingredients:

1 1/4 cups all-purpose flour
1/4 cup white sugar
2 tsps. baking powder
1 tsp. ground nutmeg
1/2 cup very thick eggnog
1/2 cup milk
1 egg, beaten
1 tbsp. oil

Directions:

1. Sift and stir flour, sugar, baking powder, and nutmeg together in a bowl.
2. Whisk eggnog, milk, egg, and oil together in a separate bowl.
3. Pour eggnog mixture into flour mixture and stir until batter is moistened and slightly lumpy.
4. Heat a lightly oiled griddle over medium-high heat, about 350 degrees F (175 degrees C).
5. Drop batter by large spoonfuls onto the griddle and cook until bubbles form and the edges are dry, 3 to 4 minutes.
6. Flip and cook until browned on the other side, 2 to 3 minutes.
7. Repeat with remaining batter.

Eggnog Cookies

Ingredients:

2 1/4 cups all-purpose flour
1 tsp. baking powder
1/2 tsp. ground cinnamon
1/2 tsp. ground nutmeg
1 1/4 cups white sugar
3/4 cup butter, softened
1/2 cup eggnog
1 tsp. vanilla extract
2 egg yolks
1 tsp. ground nutmeg

Directions:

1. Preheat oven to 325 degrees F (165 degrees C).
2. Combine flour, baking powder, cinnamon, and nutmeg.
3. Mix well with a wire whisk and set aside.
4. Cream sugar and butter until it forms a grainy paste.
5. Stir in eggnog, vanilla, and egg yolks.
6. Beat at medium speed until smooth.
7. Add flour mixture and beat at low speed just until combined.
8. Drop cookie dough by rounded teaspoonfuls onto ungreased baking sheets, 1 inch apart.
9. Sprinkle lightly with nutmeg.
10. Bake for 20 to 25 minutes, or until bottoms turn light brown.

Eggnog Cake

Ingredients:

1 (18.5 oz.) pkg. yellow cake mix
2 eggs
2 cups eggnog
1/4 cup melted butter
1/2 tsp. ground nutmeg
1/2 tsp. rum flavored extract

Filling Ingredients:

1 (3.4 oz.) pkg. instant vanilla pudding mix
2 cups eggnog
1/2 tsp. rum flavored extract

Topping Ingredients:

1 tbsp. unflavored gelatin
2 tbsps. cold water
2 cups heavy cream
1 1/4 cups sugar
1 pinch salt
1/2 tsp. rum flavored extract

Directions:

1. Preheat oven to 375 degrees F (190 degrees C).
2. Grease and flour two 8-inch round cake pans.

Cake Directions:

1. In a large mixing bowl, beat together the cake mix, eggs, 2 cups eggnog, melted butter, nutmeg, and 1/2 tsp rum flavored extract.
2. Divide the batter evenly between the two prepared cake pans.
3. Bake the cake in the preheated oven until a toothpick inserted in the center comes out clean, about 30 minutes.
4. Remove from the oven to cool on wire racks.

Filling Directions:

1. Mix together the vanilla pudding mix 2 cups eggnog, and 1/2 tsp. rum flavored extract in a medium bowl.
2. Cover with plastic wrap and refrigerate until firm, about 30 minutes.

Topping Directions:

1. In a small bowl, sprinkle gelatin over the cold water, allow to stand for 5 minutes to soften and then stir until the gelatin is fully dissolved.
2. Whip the heavy cream in a large mixing bowl to soft peaks.
3. Add the sugar, gelatin, and 1/2 tsp. rum flavored extract, and continue whipping to stiff peaks.
4. Refrigerate until ready to use.

Cake Directions:

1. Remove the cakes from the cake pans.
2. Place one round onto a serving plate.
3. Spoon the filling onto the cake round, and spread over the cake evenly.
4. Place the second cake round on top of the filling.
5. Cover the top and sides of the layered cake with the whipped topping.
6. Refrigerate until ready to serve.

About the Author

Laura Sommers is **The Recipe Lady!**

She is a loving wife and mother who lives on a small farm in Baltimore County, Maryland and has a passion for all things domestic especially when it comes to saving money. She has a profitable eBay business and is a couponing addict. Follow her tips and tricks to learn how to make delicious meals on a budget, save money or to learn the latest life hack!

Visit her Amazon Author Page to see her latest books:

amazon.com/author/laurasommers

Visit the Recipe Lady's blog for even more great recipes and to learn which books are **FREE** for download each week:

http://the-recipe-lady.blogspot.com/

Follow the Recipe Lady on **Pinterest**:

http://pinterest.com/therecipelady1

Subscribe to The Recipe Lady blog through Amazon and have recipes and updates sent directly to your Kindle:

The Recipe Lady Blog through Amazon

Laura Sommers is also an Extreme Couponer and Penny Hauler! If you would like to find out how to get things for **FREE** with coupons or how to get things for only a **PENNY**, then visit her couponing blog **Penny Items and Freebies**

http://penny-items-and-freebies.blogspot.com/

Other Books by Laura Sommers

- **Christmas Stuffing Recipes**
- **Christmas Hot Chocolate Recipes**
- **Christmas Cookies**
- **Candy Corn Cookbook**
- **Halloween Recipes**
- **50 Pumpkin Recipes**
- **Recipes for Leftover Thanksgiving or Christmas Turkey**

May all of your meals be a banquet
with good friends and good food.

Made in the USA
Lexington, KY
14 June 2019